What I Know

I KNOW FRUITS AND VEGETABLES

By Colin Matthews

Gareth Stevens PUBLISHING

first concepts

I know fruits!
These are apples.

These are bananas.

These are grapes.

These are oranges.

These are strawberries.

I know vegetables!
These are carrots.

This is broccoli.

This is lettuce.

These are beans.

These are peppers.

What fruits and vegetables do you like best?

Please visit our website, www.garethstevens.com. For a free color catalog of all our high-quality books, call toll free 1-800-542-2595 or fax 1-877-542-2596.

Cataloging-in-Publication Data

Names: Matthews, Colin.
Title: I know fruits and vegetables / Colin Matthews.
Description: New York : Gareth Stevens Publishing, 2018. | Series: What I know
Identifiers: ISBN 9781482462937 (pbk.) | ISBN 9781482462951 (library bound) | ISBN 9781482462944 (6 pack)
Subjects: LCSH: Fruit–Juvenile literature. | Vegetables–Juvenile literature.
Classification: LCC TX397.M38 2018 | DDC 363.19'2–dc23

First Edition

Published in 2018 by
Gareth Stevens Publishing
111 East 14th Street, Suite 349
New York, NY 10003

Designer: Sarah Liddell
Editor: Therese Shea

Photo credits: Cover, p. 1 (stripes) Eky Studio/Shutterstock.com; cover, p. 1 (main) monticello/Shutterstock.com; p. 3 SherSor/Shutterstock.com; p. 5 effe45/Shutterstock.com; p. 7 George Dolgikh/Shutterstock.com; p. 9 Jochen Schoenfeld/Shutterstock.com; p. 11 GooDween/Shutterstock.com; p. 13 Daria Medvedeva/Shutterstock.com; p. 15 Brent Hofacker/Shutterstock.com; p. 17 Ekaterina Kondratova/Shutterstock.com; p. 19 Ivaschenko Roman/Shutterstock.com; p. 21 Preeyaporn Srijampa/Shutterstock.com; p. 23 Bogdan Wankowicz/Shutterstock.com.

Printed in the United States of America

CPSIA compliance information: Batch #CS17GS: For further information contact Gareth Stevens, New York, New York at 1-800-542-2595.